Mirrors of Time

Other poetry titles by Barbara Gianquitto

4:04AM Thoughts

Awakening of the Heart

Mirrors of Time

Poems about soulmate love across time and space

Barbara Gianquitto

Mirrors of Time

ISBN 978-1-7395880-4-5

Illustrations and cover by Doodle Press Ltd
Foreword by Stefanie Briar

Love is not created, nor destroyed

it simply is

and it lives here

forever immortalised in the pages of this book

Contents

Foreword

by Stefanie Briar

Love has the potential to be a metaphysical experience: a sacred place where the earth and the stars collide. If fate allows, we meet a love that awakens us and takes us far beyond ourselves. "Mirrors of Time" chronicles this journey as though the universe itself is holding the pen. There are highs which are so sublime that they nearly defy description, and lows that plunge one into a true dark night of the soul. Come what may, to love this deeply eternally changes one's chemical makeup.

What sets the book you hold in your hands apart from others is that no stone is left unturned. This is not a collection of cliches about ordinary, run-of-the-mill love that could have been written by anyone. This is the result of an open soul spilling itself free across the page. It is an ode, a reckoning, an open vein, and true surrender. "Mirrors of Time" understands what often goes forgotten: love is not the absence of fear, but the ultimate act of "knowing". That concept of "knowing" is interwoven through it all: that no matter what pain, trials, or setbacks may come, the soul contract stands untouched.

There is an awareness here: a recognition of spirit that occurs when twin flames collide. The wheels of these connections are divinely orchestrated, and they continue turning for all of time, transcending even death. This is perhaps best represented by this passage from page 60:

"Distance becomes irrelevant when we are not together; I carry you with me through time and space".

Rare is the writer who can break your heart on one page and mend it on the next. Barbara does this with a deftness and beauty that will leave you in awe. More than a book, this is the complete journey of a love that absolutely no force could ever hope to separate. Open your heart, turn the page, and enjoy this epic, cosmic dance through love across the ages.

Introduction

"You want to know what God is?" – she asked as she opened her eyes after 21 hours of being in a coma.

"It is *love*. It is you, it is me. It is *us* in the Universe".

I couldn't quite grasp the words nor the meaning. I know she had been travelling far, and I knew then she was back for a reason.

"There were a million lights, the warmth was overwhelming, there was love everywhere. And it was radiating through all the lights. I could hear the colours and smell the images. Then the light opened up again, I could hear you calling me, and I came back for you. Tell me, why do we run so much here on Earth? Why do we go a million miles an hour? There is no point, my child. We are just children playing here on Earth, away from home. The Universe."

Nearly 9 years later, I find myself drawn to write about it, to study cases of Near Death experiences, of past lives and travels across dimensions.

I had been asking myself all my life what my purpose really was. Why was I here? I am sure you have already at some point in your life, too.

My mother's death was pivotal to unlocking the courage to look deeper and further.

I have read many books and studies and literature from Dr. Brian Weiss, Dr. Newton's incredible research about life between lives, and the pivotal work of Janny Juddly in "You Can Remember Who You Were Before Life Made You Forget". In this research, I was always looking for either a personal experience or seeking a psychotherapy angle to quantum physics.

I've always been drawn to the possibility that there was "more". I always felt I was "more", and yet I never quite fit in this journey on earth that started about forty years ago. It was not until much later in life when I began to put the pieces of this gigantic puzzle together.

I had glimpses of my mission here on Earth, the one I had forgotten when I incarnated into this body (the inevitable amnesia that precedes the remembering).
I had several past life regressions: I saw images of what other lives taught me and, somehow, I know that one of my main goals and missions is to understand how soulmates travel and find each other across lifetimes.

I have always had a sense of missing something, someone important. A deep search for a long-lost love.

There are some images from one past life that are burned in my soul like a movie I had seen a thousand times.

And I keep writing poetry about it, from the separation to the moment we get back home playing with the stars, to when we say goodbye to go back to Earth once more.

Promising to find each other again, to continue our journey and walk each other home again.

The search resides in this present life, in the very pages of this book which offers a different perspective.

What if there was a plan?

What if it wasn't an external, anonymous source that made such a plan. Rather, it was us who agreed to everything we are experiencing right now?

Would we look differently at all the heartbreak and pain? Would we be angry and reject the idea altogether? Who would choose to be in pain? Who would choose to have a family ending in divorce?

But what if that was just a building block, a stepping stone? Would we take a deeper breath and a few steps back to look at our life in a different way?

What if the labyrinth we think we are living in was the most beautiful tapestry, only we couldn't see the bigger picture yet?

What if all the heartbreaks and pain have just paved the way for our soul to learn, to evolve, to walk back home whole? What if without heartbreak we simply couldn't find our soulmate?

I have taken my past life experiences and weaved them with my present life, analysing all the failed relationships and heartbreaks to really see the journey of finding my soul companion I lost eons ago, and weaved them into this book of poetry. From shattering heartbreak to immense love, this book offers a journey which I hope will help you ponder and reflect on your own and look at your pain through a different lens. It is my hope that when you feel like everything is lost, you may lean into faith, whatever that word means to you. Faith in God, in the Universe, in the Light, in a Higher Force, in You.

You are the universe, you are the light, and you are your own God. And Love is just there, on the other side of pain, waiting for you with open arms.

I promise.

Part 1

Broken Mirrors

Before Us

Mirrors of Time

I am afraid of the coldness my soul is in.
I keep looking for the fire,
for the light,
for the warmth,
for the soul companion I lost eons ago
in a heart-shattering loss.
I cannot rest until I find you again.
I keep looking in the woods,
in the forests,
in the remote corners of the Universe,
in the black holes of the mirrors of time.
Painfully and frantically searching
like I promised you,
in the last words that left my dying breath.
This ache transcends time and space;
it has no logic.
And every time I think I've found you
– and life reminds me that I was wrong –
I lose you all over again.

Intuition

"You have no idea of what amazing things are going to happen",
said no-one with no words or any sounds of sorts.
Intuition has this strange habit of humming inside my body

as it travels to my ears.
I stop doing the dishes and look up.
It is an inner-knowing, a sense of divine timing,

a passenger of realms.
It is not a voice, but it is firm
and loving.

The vibrations move to my throat
and I am compelled to say out loud:

"I'll wait, I promise".

The ache

You are the ache I feel
every time my mind wanders
back to you.

Salt on skin

I don't have the right shoes
to walk on such salty roads.
There is only sorrow in my eyes.
I step forward, just to please you.

At your mercy: *expectations.*

Grief leaves me exposed
like a tree in winter.
Everything is sinking in salt
burning on my flesh.

Will it destroy me?

Or will it finally heal me?

We are done

She was only a little girl
wanting to give you a flower.
She placed it right in your hands –

the same hands that bruised my arm.

You didn't even turn around.
"It's because we have broken up" – I hear in the distance
(as if a little girl would understand).

But you did. And you chose to walk away.

"We are done", I whisper
behind my breath,
then louder,

then screaming:

"We are done".

A poet's heart

Be careful falling in love with a poet
for she will describe in hues of longing your every sigh,
on a canvas of feelings you can never quite get the full
picture of.

She will paint in words the shades of silence
in a million different ways, how your eyes follow her
every movement until you reach out to kiss her.

She will capture the essence
of the smallest of moments as if she could stop time.

She will describe how her heart was racing
in the absence of the words she longed to hear,
as the desert begs for water.

She will trap every emotion
in immortal verses of poetry
in a sunset that can never end.

She will make art from your love
in ways you have never seen before.

But be careful breaking a poet's heart
for her words will cut every piece of paper she will ever
touch, and your eyes will weep at the sight of every
piece of her broken heart.

For even poetry itself will bleed for eternity.

Like glass under my feet

Another ending on the horizon,
struggling to see the gift of new beginnings,
yet my throat is on fire.
Numbness is all I can feel;
I so wanted it to be you.
I hear footsteps leaving,
crushing glass under each step,
away from the door,
miles from safety.
They say "*Have courage*".
They say "*Have faith*".
How can breaking a heart ever be okay?
Guilt makes way into my body like liquid fire
from throat to lungs.

I am the one closing the door.
The footsteps leaving
are m i n e.

Strangers once again

I have no doubt you were my soulmate.
Did we really meet at the wrong time?

My words are lost in a silent space.
I still remember how you smiled,
the way you held my hand and moved me

on the other side of the pavement,
away from the cars to keep me safe,
but the future we had planned is now an illusion.

Memories haunt me and as they move,
bruising my soul at each breath.
There.is.no.more.time.
no more smiles.

You took it all away,
and I still don't know why.

The door of pain

All my insecurities are pounding at my door.
Screaming unwelcoming words,
pushing through a door that is not strong enough.

I so want to open that door and ask them to leave.

Instead, I sink on the floor, and
rest my back against this wooden door.
Hoping my tears will muffle

the sound of my own mind.

In search of lost time

I hear a memory coming up
from a great distance:
strong, fast, melancholic.

I can almost taste it in my mouth.
It never gets any easier to swallow,
bitter like the time I had to say goodbye.

Sweet like the memory of our eyes
locking in for the last time.
Strong like the arms that used to hold me.

This time will never come back,
not in this life.
I can only ever see you

when I smell the sweet
scent of jasmine.
I choose to allow the memories to wash over

my body like a salty ocean wave
until the time I'll see your beautiful
eyes again.

No longer us

Is that all it was?
        What was that no longer is?
I feel you slipping away
        like water trickling down my fingers
        I can't catch you, not anymore.
        The more I try, the less I have a grip.
I used to love how I was the only one who could
        make sense of your restless mind
        and make friends with your demons.
Tell me I am wrong,
        tell me it is just a bad dream.
Tell me you won't let fear win, again.
        Tell me you still see me.
        Tell me you still see *us*.

Unlove you

I didn't unlove you overnight.
It was the way we had to weather more winters than
springs, leaving splinters in my heart
impossible to remove u n s c a t h e d.

It was the shutting down on the days the bed was half *empty*,
when words refused to leave the chambers
of your throat to save us.

It was the way you didn't miss me,
and all the ways you didn't love me in the way
I knew you could.

It was the way I saw our distorted image in
the mirror of a time I thought was ours.

I didn't unlove you overnight:
It happened s l o w l y,
then quickly,
then all.at.once.

The glue

Sometimes things just break.

You – only seeing the finality of it.

Me – sitting with all the glue in the world in my hands.

But I can't move – and you can't see it.

Haunted

I am in a haunted house. I was brought here, not sure by whom. I am afraid. I see stairs, I am afraid of the dark, the cold. I need light, air, and warmth.

Where are the blankets?

My nostrils are burning from the smell of damp and wet. No-one is here. I am afraid of my own company. I am afraid I can't save myself this time. Or have I ever been able to?

Can I abandon this haunted heart of mine? Why can't I simply get out?

There aren't any chains, only doors. And all doors are open.
They've always been open.
Just one breath, just one step.

I am the only one holding me hostage.

Standing at the edge

I am standing at the edge of the end. At the end of new beginnings.

I've tiptoed around myself for far too long. I feel my wings are cutting my skin so deep in order to be freed. There is a pool of blood and feathers at my bare feet. I stand naked before a new version of myself, and I squint my eyes to focus on this new image forming. Somewhere between a phoenix and a human. It's too big to fit in a mere mirror, yet still too small to contain these wings. How do I even use them? How do I fly when I still feel so heavy?

I'm standing at the edge of the end, blood cleansing my soul. I bathe in the light of the moon; I burn in its energy.

I'm standing at the edge of something new, something that has been hiding behind the gates of a heaven
I never believed in.

"*Where am I going?*" my inner voice asks for no-one to hear. I can't see the road, there are just open doors in the middle of a forest; I don't know where they lead nor which one to step through.

"*Where am I going?*"

A silent voice hums in my throat, seeps through my veins and reaches my ears:

"*Where you were always meant to:*
Just go."

Uninvited visitor

Sadness came to greet me today – she was utterly uninvited, but she took no notice of my protests. She sat down and put the bags of tears on the floor. She stared deep down into my eyes. She never spoke a word. I know all she wanted was to be held.

So I held her, and whispered:
"Hello, sadness. Are you here to stay long?"

She never replied, but she wept each and every one of the tears she carried until there was none left. Until we both finally fell asleep.

Unripe

I envy the birds:
how they rest on the branches
and observe everything from a distance.

I am tired of being everyone's someone,
I want to have the space to be no-one
until I figure out who I want to be

to everyone.

I want to sleep and rest,
yet I am so tired of resting.
I am so exhausted from being exhausted.

I often wonder where you are, my love.
I wonder what am I doing here without you
and the answer changes every time.

When the past rings its bell,

it's not always an invitation to

step back and re-evaluate.

It is the Universe asking you:

"Have you learned your lesson"?

I will not tell you

Today I will not say I am okay. Instead I will tell you that I am trying. Trying to keep going and put one foot in front of the other. That I only cried twice today and I feel this is progress.

Today I will not say I am okay to the world and all my friends who are supporting me. Instead, I will tell you that sadness is leaving space for anger and I am seething through my teeth at how unfair I feel this all is.

Today I will not say I am okay, I will tell you I am tying my hands behind my back not to reach out to you like I want to, just to tell you "*I miss you*".

Today I will not say I am okay, but I will tell you I am feeling a fraction better and I am scared of it. I am afraid I will no longer remember the sound of my name falling off your lips.

And I am petrified I will be okay with it.

The door

I open the door once again;
my heart atrophies like a stone
left to rot at the bottom of the sea.
I open the door once again;
a gentle breeze comes in
whispering secrets I cannot yet comprehend.
You stand before me:
soul naked, soft, vulnerable,
so beautiful.
I open the door once again:
there are no fairies hiding anymore
in the thick fog that once gave me so much peace.
And if I am once again at the bottom of the sea
I want to know why:

Why *did* I open that door again?

Unrequited

It's time I take a long walk into the dark paths of my mind.
Feet bare, cold grass. Even the birds are not singing their chorus today.
The trees show me a path of shadows I must go through.

It's hard to know when to stop and when to carry on; if the seeds will grow into sweet red cherries, or if the stars will hold on for a while longer. They say we must go and see this through, like a pull giving into the gravity.

It's cold here and yet a calming silence washes over me.
My limbs are tired, my heart is heavy to carry around.
Grief has never left, like a homeless tenant with a life-long unpaid rental contract that I cannot evict.

It's a pain that has its roots deep into the Universe. I carry it in my soul, looking for answers to questions posed in other lives. I seem to continue a relentless search for my long-lost love.

And at times, my unrequited soul is at peace, it feels like it found its lost home again,
but walls become smaller and windows begin to break,
brick cracks, and the Earth doesn't feel stable anymore.

I close my eyes as I have learned to breathe. I wait until it passes through my body and – as it does – grief bruises my bones and keeps leaving marks in my aching soul.
I get glimpses of answers only in my dreams.

Fields of lavender and robins singing a sweet melody that calms my soul.
They show me a house full of love that I only see in the reflection of his eyes staring at me with adoring wonder.

Those blue eyes I get to see only in my dreams. No wonder I want to sleep so I can see them again. Waiting until night gives way to the stars, and the shadows encapsulate me once more, so I can see the light again.

Restless souls

And I retreat in poetry:
in words and rhymes,
my existence seeping through the ink,
too big for the page, too small to take its rightful space.
I don't know why it always works:
the surrender to the pain,
the joy,
the not-knowing.
I guess that's why poets are always
r e s t l e s s souls.

If it's not worth your breath,

it deserves your silence.

I want

A love that looks for me in every song,
a collision of stars in every universe,
the omega to every alpha,

a last ending.

Gains and losses

I ache at how much I miss you when you're next to me.
How I am unable to access the parts of you I once had freely, when everything was new and time was created, when space didn't exist, and the universe was made only by our breaths.

As time goes by, I say goodbye to the million versions of ourselves I once loved that no longer are.

Grief is the only way to make space
for the new ones that are yet to emerge.

And this is the thing with love: the acceptance that losses are in equal parts to gains.

Loving you

It was like a reckless hike on the highest mountain.
        The one with the prettiest of views.
Never once wondering how we would ever get down safely.
        The most beautiful adventure I have ever lived.
Only our feet were deep in the snow with
        temperature below freezing,
no gloves or hats on.
        How beautiful it was: the thought
that only *l o v e* would always keep us safe and warm.

I am

I am chaos and calm,
    wildflower and hurricane,
    gentle river flow and raging waves.
I am flames and rain,
    loud words and terrifying silences,
    tears and joy forever weaved together.

But most of all I am love.

    I am all *l o v e.*

I have been hiding

I have been hiding in self-judgment and shame,
under grief and tears, in a place I didn't know
I could ever come out alive from.

I have been hiding where the sky meets the horizon:
where nobody could ever fully reach me
under galaxies not born yet.

I have been hiding in a place
between longing and belonging
unseen, un-heard: the only space I felt safe.

I have been hiding for an eternity;
that is no longer welcome.

Life lesson

You weren't meant to stay.
As much as I wanted to hold onto you,
as much as my soul recognised yours
remembering glimpses of a past life together,
in this life you were just my
life lesson.

Everything for you

I would have
moved oceans and mountains to keep you safe,
stripped the Earth of its primordial fire to keep you
warm, asked the rain to stop knocking on your window
so you could sleep.
I could have
been the song you escaped to when you felt sad,
the safe shore in the stormiest of waters,
the ending of any new beginnings.
But fear won – and I have to see you go
with the pieces of my heart you promised
you'd never let go.

Nothing or anything

We were everything in a world that gave us absolutely nothing.

Our love was way too big for our human bodies to contain; it spilled in an overflowing river that took us under.

And I watch the water carrying you away from me, drowning all our dreams along with what's left of us.

There are no branches to hold on to. There is no salvation, only the reluctant surrender to an ending I never saw coming.

Don't let go

I don't want space.

I want you to obsess over how easily you have left and regret it. I want the thought of me to wash over you in all the million ways you didn't give us a chance to make this better.

I don't want silence. I want to hear the knock on my door and pebbles thrown at my window. I want your tears to mix with mine until it is all we can drink.

I want to collapse in your arms knowing that – this time – you won't let me go.

Birds do sing in the rain

I have slept in your T-shirt even though it doesn't have your smell anymore. The room is silent and all I can hear are the birds. It is raining outside, I guess we have finally proven that birds *do* sing in the rain.
I envy them, you know? The ability to sing despite the rain pouring down.
I keep looking at the phone waiting for something and there is nothing. I simply cannot let you go – too much left undone, too much love trapped in this chest. I can't fix what I haven't broken and that's the worst part: I can't do anything about it.
But I can't do this nothingness, and certainly not so abruptly. We crashed and burned in flames that were way too high; we kept feeding them insecurities instead of patience and kindness until they spread even further and took you under. I was standing at the top, lending you a hand to pull you out – the same hand you used to lay on your heart when we used to breathe together.

I could scream a million times "*Come back to me, my love*",
but the birds are singing, and the rain is heavy,
and you are too far away to hear me.

Breathe with me

Come closer,
whisper words I can believe
until I can trust again.
Breathe with me;
sink into the new sunrise
knowing you won't let go
of all the images and promises.
I am so tired of letting you go
if only in my mind.

The wind will carry a message for you

I wish you could feel my whispers each morning when I wake up.
I still say good morning to a silent phone.
I still reach out to message you, only it ends up in my notes.
I wonder if you can feel it somehow, my hurt and my longing for you.
I can only ask the wind to carry it for me,
so whenever you feel a breeze against your cheek,
please know this is me caressing your face
with all of the love that is still here, trapped,
waiting for you to *come back*.

Rest

I sit quietly by the sea.
The sun is peeping through the horizon clouds,
and I drink it in until my soul feels warm again.
Only the wind is whispering to the ocean waves,
and my heart listens to an ancient language I cannot yet comprehend.
But somehow today, it's enough.
It's okay if I don't understand; there is a time for everything.
In perfect stillness, in harmonious silence.
Even my demons are resting.

Surrender

What if the scariest thing was the stepping stone you needed to fly?
What if you could re-frame that fear into opportunity?
What if we could just surrender to the Universe and the journey?
What if you could trust that you are exactly where you are meant to be?
What if you needed those shadows to wrap around you like a blanket so you could rest?
What if this stillness was the only progress you needed?

What if, in the absence of words, you could finally find your voice?

The liminal space

I thought about you today, and it didn't rip my heart out.
I have been able to breathe without crying, and I
didn't feel like the earth was swallowing me whole.

I am happy, for now, to stay in this place in between:
The liminal space between the memories of what was
and a future that no longer is.

House of Cards

I've been thinking a lot lately about what happened, looking for ways to fill this silence that is around me.

I still think of your smile and how good it felt (at the beginning).

How you held my daughters and for the first time I thought "*Wow, there are men out there that are really amazing, how lucky am I?*"

So I built dreams in a house that had small foundations on unsolid ground, but it didn't matter. There was so much love that I wanted so desperately to believe. Believe in the way you showed up and loved me in the best way you knew how – how you needed me to hold you and all your broken pieces. It was my job, wasn't it? It was my job to fix you, and I forgot what I was breaking to make space for you. I didn't see how I was splitting myself in half to give you what you needed.

I've been thinking a lot lately about what happened. About the ways we laughed until our bellies hurt, and we had tears in our eyes, and we thought we were invincible. Making a million reckless plans without stopping for a second to breathe and check in – running like children to catch a rainbow that was too far away. When we sang in the car at the top of our lungs and nothing else mattered but our breath, our hands holding, and the wind in our face.

But the wind changed and swept you away from me, overnight, in the blink of an eye, the dreaded five words "I can't do this anymore" – all gone in a puff of smoke. There was no discussion, nor reasoning, nor empathy of any sorts. You were gone, and I was left to pick up the pieces of a destruction I didn't see coming. And it doesn't matter how many times I ask myself what I have done wrong. Because the truth is: absolutely nothing, if not losing myself in a version of me I thought was more loveable. The version of me that tries too hard to be loved. The version of me I swore one too many times I wouldn't become again.

The version of me I now leave buried in the past, with you.

You will wonder about me

You will wonder about me, many times.
You will ask yourself why silence is all there is.

There will be times you'll wonder
how I am and if I'm still grieving your loss.

There will be times you will tell yourself you hope
I am doing OK.

You will miss me at times, I am sure.
You'll keep telling yourself a million stories
to feel at peace with yourself.

You'll keep wondering,
and I'll keep my *silence.*

I release you

You came into my life like an unexpected ray of sunshine in a cold winter, and you left as unexpectedly as the biggest explosion, setting everything on fire.

I loved you more than I thought I would ever be capable of, and I think part of me always will, but you weren't mine to keep, and I wasn't yours to hold.

I hope time will make me remember the way I felt in your arms. I hope it will wash away the hurt and the memories of the last words that cut me so deep, faced with a change I never saw coming yet – somehow – inevitable, like the change of a season.

As we become strangers once again, as all evidence that we ever existed gets erased, I ache at every splinter that gets removed from my skin.

The truth is, I don't want to hold onto any resentment anymore. There must be a reason for all of this; I believe there are lessons for both of us in this. And the answers will come when the time is right.

And so today I release you: from my thoughts, from my energy, and from my heart.

I won't look for you in all the signs around me anymore, I won't use you as a wish every time an eyelash falls in my hands. I won't look for you in my dreams when I close my eyes. I need to make space. I need to make space for wholeness.

I hope you find the light, and when you do, I hope you will have enough courage to hold onto it without an ounce of indecision in your heart.

I wish you nothing but happiness.
That's all I ever wanted for you.

A piece of my heart will always be with you

I have grown accustomed to silence,
in fact I crave it these days.
I go to bed early and switch off my phone.

I don't worry about anything else but myself:
my breath, my bones, my soul.

I still think of you from time to time;
I think part of me always will.

Do you remember when I told you that a piece of my heart
was yours, when you used to hold me tight
as if the world didn't exist?

You never gave it back;
it wasn't packed with the things you sent me.

And I am happy it is still with you.
Love is not created, nor destroyed: it simply is.

But I have grown accustomed to silence
and it doesn't terrify me anymore.

I have made friends with myself, and I feel like
I am finally in good company.

Just me and the notion that I am more than enough.
I finally see it.

If there is medicine in heartbreak;
this has been the cure.

What a gift.
What a gift indeed.

There is nothing more poetic

than listening to my reflection

softly whispering:

"You are doing just fine".

Robin

I sit by the river,
listening closely to how
the wind whispers secrets to the trees.

I watch the water carrying fleeting pieces of truth
I can't quite grasp yet.
A robin hums quietly before

taking off in the hot breeze of summer,
reminding me that I carry the entire universe
in the palms of my hands.

Never too much

I want a soulmate love
the "*where have you been my whole life*" love

I want the "*thank you for trusting me with your tears*" love
the one that is so deeply ripped in trust
where there is not one ounce of anxiety
or second-guessing.

I want the "*let me watch you sleep and make sure we have settled the argument before bed*" love
the one that asks me how I am twice just to make sure
I know there's real space to open up.

I want the forever love that I can taste on my lips
every time I call his name
and it's never "*too much*".

Part 2

Time Together

On Earth

The early days of winter

All the leaves have fallen
like my old dreams
and small aspirations.

I step on them, crushing them under my feet
like old glass shattered in a million pieces.

The road is white like my cat's fur,
and I can't help but take it all in,
finally breathing freely.

The new lights shining on the old
Christmas tree that I never change each year
remind me that there is beauty in change.

This house has now finally become a home
and I am not afraid of a bed I share on my own.
The promise of a new beginning now shines bright
ahead of me.

And I hope I will be brave enough
to grasp it without indecision
on my hands.

Homecoming

I don't recognise the body you have in in this life,
nor your voice or the way you move.
I don't recognise anything except the way you look at me.

The way your soul calls to mine,
the way my soul responds beyond human comprehension.
When the world stops and I find myself in a forever

that I have been missing for so long.
The sense of safety is almost overwhelming.
But with you, I know now:

it's an old forever,
it's a "*Hello again*",
it's a *h o m e c o m i n g*.

Waiting for you

I sit here waiting for you,
the you I don't yet know,
the you I feel pulled towards.

The image of you washes over me
like jasmine petals with
the sweetest, delicate scent.

I remember how your smile
made my soul notice
a new electricity.

I long for your hands to touch mine,
for my name to fall off your lips,
for you to press on my body leaving an
imprint on my soul.

I long for seeds to blossom
into a strong oak tree
with roots stronger than the Earth.

The warmth of winter

I lay in bed under the pink and grey fluffy covers I got for my birthday. My cat is purring next to me; its white fur blends perfectly with the covers, and I smile. It feels like my covers are purring and sharing a sense of contentment.

It wasn't too long ago when I felt so different, laying in the same bed, with the same fluffy covers drenched in my tears, all my unmet expectations sitting next to me, broken like an unfolded origami that never quite made it.

But winter is here and I am warm again. It's strange, isn't it, how the absence of warmth makes you burn for it?
The grey and pink walls are home to the big clock standing before me that I love so much. It is stuck at the thirteenth hour, and I never want it to start again.

So I press my face deeper into the warm pink pillowcase as the cat stretches a bit more into the blanket. I close my eyes thinking of you, and the more I try, the less I can sleep.

This unfamiliar sense of joy is making all those damn butterflies dance again.

Consume me

You consume my every waking thought,
my nights, my dreams,
my every fibre at a molecular level.

I don't know how this has happened.
My whole body feels different
like a magnetic pull, my soul calls yours.

I feel I had known you before I knew you;
I had felt you before I could feel you.
I had loved you before I fell in love with you.

You feel like a fragile creature waiting
for a love that has never arrived
until now.

A complex soul waiting to be seen, finally for the first time
the most infinite source of light and love,
caged for too long in darkness, held hostage by demons.

A heart that is larger than life whose pieces are scattered
around,
like a puzzle waiting to be put back together.
I feel like I have called you from a remote corner of the
Universe,

and you have answered.
I am *finally* holding you.
Welcome home, my love.

I have missed you.

Don't say you love me

Please don't say you love me. Not before you have seen how grumpy I am in the morning before my coffee. Not before you see how sometimes I have no patience, and get frustrated at my children not listening when I ask them to do things a million times.

Please don't say you love me, not before I tell you about how my heart has been crushed, and lied to, and betrayed. Not before I tell you how I cried and implored the gods to bring back the one I loved so dearly. The one who left the day after telling me I was where he belonged.

Please don't say you love me if you don't get curious about what I truly believe in and stand for. If you haven't seen the chaos I can bring when my shadows are dancing around me, refusing to be ignored.

Please don't say you love me if we have only had good and fun times at the beginning and everything is seen through rose tinted glasses. That's the easy part.

Please don't say you love me if you haven't really seen me, for who I truly am and not for who you want me to be. If you are not ready to have deep conversations about our values and what we both bring to the table, real, raw and true conversations.

Say you love me when you can see through me and feel how love seeps through my veins in a way that's hard to contain; tell me you are ready to embrace it. Tell me you accept my shadows as much as my light.

And then, and only then, I will believe it.

And I promise: my heart will be y o u r s.

Distance is not relevant

You are bringing me back to life:
a new life,
our life.

I haven't slept or eaten properly
since I met you,
since our eyes first locked, and

our hands touched, and
we couldn't let go.
And as much as you hold me,

it is never quite close enough,
I want to jump out of my skin
and fuse into you.

Our eyes laugh together before our
mouths do,
there is a sense of overwhelming

familiarity that has taken me under.
I listen to the million stories and
hundreds of names of all the people

you want me to meet that I'll never
remember, and I am completely lost
in how beautiful your eyes are when

you are happy.

Distance becomes irrelevant when
we are not together;
I carry you with me through time and
space.

I didn't know I wanted you

You are everything I didn't know I wanted.
I didn't know I could feel anything anymore
beyond the fear of falling and being hurt.

I didn't know I'd surrender to those beautiful
eyes beyond reasonable human
comprehension.

Maybe it was the way you held my hand
for those few seconds more
than we should have.

Maybe it was the way you hugged me
so tight I felt I could melt into you,
or the way you laughed when we talked about Venice.

Or the way your soul touched mine,
like a quiet humming vibrating
from my ears to my heart.

I didn't know I wanted you
until I met you.

I didn't know that everything I felt before you
wasn't even a fraction of what
I *could* feel.

Everything I've ever known,
simply wasn't anymore,
and I have never been so happy to be wrong.

December night

It wasn't just a hug on that cold December night.
It was the biggest and warmest embrace of my soul,
our hearts finally close enough.

You held me for what felt like an eternity
and I breathed – so deeply – resting my head on your chest,
lost in your strong arms, somehow it felt like I was finally
found.

Then I looked up, and I saw how beautifully
the light of the full moon was reflecting
in your deep, blue eyes.

The longing in that moment of silence
took my breath away.
and I k n e w

that all I needed was to kiss you.
After searching for eons,
I was exactly where I had been longing for:
home.

A perfect morning

Stirring in bed welcoming a new dawn,
all I can think about is coffee and you.
The covers are still warm from us.

You smile at how perfectly I fit
in the space between your neck and shoulder,
and even better when I rest my head on your chest.

You hold me tight and we just listen
to the beauty of the silence around us,
just the sound of our heartbeats is enough.

Breathing like it was the first time.
I don't need to open my eyes to know that
you are smiling. I can't think of a more
perfect way to start the day.

Not normal

You won't find anything normal here:
    Just a naked soul wearing nothing
but the truth.
    Enough madness to make you
question: what have you been doing without me
    all your damn life?

A whole new world

I hope you know how much you mean to me.
I hope you know that when I close my eyes at night,
you're the only one I still see

oh so clearly.

I hope you know you have turned my world upside down,
and for the first time it feels like it's in the right place.
I hope you know that I feel you running through my veins

in a way that I can't explain, but it makes a world of sense.
I hope you know that when you look at me time stops,
nothing else exists,

only those eyes
that voice
and, *my god*,

that beautiful face.

Sunday Morning

The bed is still warm and I am taking a moment to breathe
through this wave of emotions.
Of the unspoken promise of a new tomorrow:
we talk without talking.
Words make a dance of their own,
back and forth.
Your smile carries them until they swirl
with loaded pauses and loud silences
Smiles and sweet kisses,
hearts beating fast with anticipation and fear.
On the edge of jumping into something new,
holding onto our breath.
Suffocating in the last hug,
resting my head between your shoulder and neck.
I don't want you to leave;
keep holding me.

The colour of your name

Every time you look at me,
you take a little bit more
of my darkness
a w a y.

Your light, finally free to shine again,
is pouring out from every fibre
of your being.
It's *intoxicating*.

You hold me like the flame holds the
campfire wood, and I can't
move away from the warmth.
The fire is cocooning me,

and I've never felt safer.

You draw me in like a slow dance;
I can't resist losing myself in it.
You hold my pieces together like
they've never been broken.

So I paint the colour of your name

in shades of longing and devotion,
on a blank canvas made of forgotten
dreams you are now bringing back to life.

You make real what I thought I had lost forever,
what I didn't think I could feel again,
weaving in hues of hope and yearning.

And I'll keep painting until
all the colours have set and the picture is clear:
the image of a new beginning
that we are embracing with no hesitations,
with hearts open, ready to love again.

Maybe forever is just not long enough.

Like a prayer

I love how I can feel you smiling even when
I have my eyes closed,

how time and space have no meaning
when we are together,

lost in our universe
yet found in a new definition of love.

But most of all, I love how you
hold my name under your breath,

like an exhale,
like a sigh,
like a prayer.

Catch me when I fall

How long does it take to fall in love?
A moment in your arms,
a look that reaches my soul,

the flaps of the wings of a butterfly?

How long does it take? A minute, a day, a lifetime?
Hearts beating faster, longing to be in your arms,
in the certainty of our tomorrow.

For the first time, I am not anxious.

I am certain you will catch me.
I know I will stumble,
but I am not afraid of the fall.

I know you will be there.
You already are.
How long does it take to fall in love?

Can it be the split second of our lips touching,
and our souls smiling,
whispering:

*"I would have waited another thousand lives
to be with you again".*

The answer

You are peeling off layers of debris from my heart.
    You are mending ancient scars,
    loving all my darkness into light.

You are the answer to a question
    I didn't know I was asking,
    the medicine I didn't know I needed,

You are.
    You simply *are*
    the light I never thought I'd see.

Melt into me

You are so beautiful when you lay yourself
bare before me;
exposed, vulnerable, soul naked.

As if my love was the purest thing you've ever seen.
As if my touch was going to heal
all your wounds.

Tomorrow

I will tell you I love you, and the world won't be the same ever again. Tomorrow I will be terrified to have those three small words leave my breath: "*I love you*". Tomorrow I will surrender to what my heart has been telling me since the day I first met you, and my universe found a new meaning. I know this world is too much for you right now; I know there is hardly any space. But I promise I will create it. I will dig the earth, and create a cave where you can breathe. I promise I will keep you safe under the rocks and leave a corner open so that enough light can always shine on you.

Tomorrow I will say *I love you* to the last person I will ever whisper these three words to.

The nectar

You make me redefine what love truly is,
what it is supposed to feel like: simple, calm, effortless,
whole.
You are the nectar my life was missing.

You are the warmth melting ancient icebergs,
you are the calm the storm in my heart
was longing for.

True love feels so simple.
And in its simplicity lies its
magnificence.

Home again

It didn't take long for our souls
to recognise each other.

"*Welcome back*",
they silently whispered
as our lips touched
for the first time
after many lifetimes.

"*I have missed you*".

Embrace

There is a way you hug me that makes me feel the safest I have ever been.
A way we breathe together and find comfort in the rising and falling of our chests.
A moment I forget the world outside even exists and I hold onto you until I can't anymore.
Because the world does exist, and we have to go back to it.
So I watch you closing the door looking at me for a second more, the longing in your eyes is achingly beautiful. I know you are leaving a piece of your heart with me, along with your essence I can still smell on my hair. I will keep it safe until I will see those beautiful eyes again, looking at me as if I am the most beautiful creature in the entire Universe.

Break open

The purity of this love
permeates ancient scars,
like warm honey filling the cracks

one by one,

restoring beliefs buried in the depths of my soul,
redefining the very essence of what love
should feel like

making my heart break,
break *o p e n.*
Leaving nothing but peace,

nothing but
wholeness.

Never close enough

You kiss me,
and all I want to do
is jump out of my skin
and melt into you.

Love fiercely,
unapologetically,
magnificently,
endlessly.

Love with all you've got.

Unconditional

You saw my scars and loved me more for each of them.
You watched me dancing with my fears,
always pulling me up each time I stumbled and fell,

drying my tears,

like a beam of warm sunshine
ducking under the waves of doubts with me
never rushing me to come up for air.

My God, you make it look so effortless
to love me unconditionally,
as if there couldn't be

any other way.

Alpha and Omega

You make me feel like this
is the beginning of

forever.

Love me

Fall in love with my soul,
with all those little things
that seem irrelevant.
These are what keep my heart
beating for you.
Fall in love with my mind;
it will lead straight to
my heart.

The answer

And then there was you:
        warm sunshine after a long winter,
            the song in my silence,

the warmth in my cold,
        the peace in my chaos,
            the colour to my grey.

You simply are
        the answer to a question
            I didn't know I was
longing for.

My Light

Can you love my darkness:
the shadows that haunt me,
the fears that taunt me,
the secrets that hurt me?

Can you love my darkness:
the scars that mark me,
the wounds that bleed me,
the pain that breaks me?

Can you love my darkness:
the way I love yours,
the way I accept yours,
the way I embrace yours?

Can you walk through my shadows,
and be my light when I cannot see?

Tell me, can you love my darkness
as much as you love me?

And when they asked me:

"What is happiness?"

I didn't think twice

before I started describing

You.

I belong to us

And no matter how long I am away
dancing with my fears,
I know you are never too far

for me to return in your arms,
the only place where
I belong.

Close to you

We are so close that I don't know if it's my breath or yours that we are breathing in. The sense of safety and grounding makes me feel I can exhale freely.

I let go by giving in. My closed fists become open palms, my jaw unclenches. I take a step forward. The water is deep, and suddenly I am not scared of the depth.

We don't need to say anything to comprehend the magnitude of these feelings. Like the wind whispers secrets to the trees that the Universe holds sacred, we become the Universe itself.

We are children of the infinite love we have been so afraid to surrender to. My heart beats like drums in a sacred ceremony I am no longer a stranger to; we feel it in our bones how the energy is locking us in.

The final redemption, the ultimate salvation.

And we feel like we finally belong.

The Moon was listening

I told the Moon about you.
I talked about your beautiful eyes
and how I feel safe in your arms.

I told her we laugh until our bellies hurt,

and about how I held you and dried your tears
that night when the world stopped,
and you felt all the pain

you never allowed yourself to feel until now.

How we talk for hours and hours and forget to breathe,
how I feel you under my tongue
like a fresh bite of a summer strawberry,

just ripe enough to drink it in.

How I feel enough when I am around you,
and I don't need to pretend to be someone else.
I told her how your hands are big enough

to contain all my contradictions,

that I don't have to make myself smaller
to fit into the origami box
where I spent most of my life.

She listened softly as she always does until she whispered
"*Can you see now?*
how the darkness led you to the most beautiful light?"

Lifeboat

You feel like a lifeboat into an ocean of doubts.
So, when you ask me what the bridge
between fear and happiness is

I can only respond:
You, my love.

You.

Fantasy and reality

For so long, I had been stuck
somewhere between fantasy and reality,
the only place I've ever
felt safe enough to dream.

That is, until I met you.
For now I dream
with my eyes wide open.

Stepping Stones

I can see now how heartbreak
was just a stepping stone,

a path made of thorns
just to get to where we were
always meant to be:

the path that led me to you.

To *us*.

A little bit of eternity

I knew I'd find you again, in this life:
after all the stars exploded,
and the Moon moved thousands of oceans.
The sense of familiarity when I look into your eyes
is overwhelming:
we have done this before, in another life.
This Love transcends space and time;
we are just traveling another dimension, my love.
Our souls recognised each other before we did.
They pulled us together again
for another little bit of
eternity.

Demons

I stand in awe of you, how you say "Hello" to my demons and
offer them a cup of tea, too. How you want to understand
where they come from and how many scars they left.
I stand in awe of how you love me
more – so much more – for each
and every one of them.

Home

My home has its roots into the Universe.
I have lived there for longer than I have lived on Earth,
standing at the edge of forever,

dancing with the stars.

I have rested in galaxies I did not know the name of
and restored my soul energy in a place
where no words were needed.

I never thought I'd find this calm again
when I left my home to come to Earth.
Yet with you, my love, I feel like I am dancing

with the stars again.

And I can't help but surrender to a new forever.

It's you

All I can see is you,
all I can feel is you.
In my head,
in my heart,
in every fibre of my being.

It's like you changed my molecular structure.

You are my eyes when I cannot see,
my ears when I cannot hear,
my voice when I cannot speak,
my light when darkness is

all there is.

A bridge into forever

I took all the stones that have ever been thrown at me,
all the ones that broke my heart,
all the ones that buried me in the land of despair.

I stacked them up, one by one, and I climbed them
until I saw the light, the warmth.
Until I saw you there,

right at the top patiently waiting for me,
with open arms and a heart that is finally
ready to love freely.

Your name

Happiness walks in softly,
caresses my ears as a delicate, white feather,

and gently, *so gently*,

whispers something that sounds a lot like
your name.

I'll be there

Tell me your secrets;
tell me everything that scares you.
Tell me how you need to be held

When you feel alone in the dark.
And I will hold you tight,
'til the sun
rises again.

The right way

You didn't steal my heart.
You left it right there where it was
and gave it the love and respect it deserved,

instead.

I am everything

I am everything that you didn't know you were looking for.
I am fire and ice,
the pebble you throw in the river
that bounces back three times.

I am solid oak roots deeply planted in the Universe
only here on Earth for a little while
to learn and grow.

I am everything that
it's difficult to forget and
impossible to love.

Unless it's unconditional and undeniable:
like the certainty of a new dawn.

Everything I need

The sun peeps at the horizon and I drink it in,
until my belly is full.
It is a beautiful day even if my email list is too long
and laundry needs to be done.
I have coffee in my veins and stars in my eyes.
And everything I'll ever need today:
I have me.
I have you.
I have *us*.

Can you sit with me

Can you sit with me
when the day is hard and I can't catch my breath,
when tears fall down my cheeks and I don't know why,
when love doesn't feel as strong as the day we met,
when I feel like evaporating into droplets of water in
the sky?

Can you sit with me
when I am afraid of losing myself again,
when I need a hug and comforting words,
when I need my hand held and permission to exhale,
when I need to breathe together with your hand
on my chest?

Can you sit with me
in the silence of a calm heartbeat,
no longer deafening with its pounding drumming,
when I tell you I don't fit in any moulds and I have big
feelings, that the world has always been scared of?

Will you sit with me and find beauty in this?
or will you see it as terrifying and run away
like everyone else?

(I really hope you stay).

Stardust and supernova

I choose you every day
over everything and everyone.
I will always choose you, my love...

in this and every life, I will keep living

just like we promised.

When we were us and didn't have any names,
when our wedding rings were made of stardust,
and the fireworks were the supernovas exploding before us,

a million years ago.

I will always choose you
in every form,
in every era

in every realm.

Our souls will always show us the way.

I just want a cup

of peppermint tea,

comforting silences,

a blanket over my legs,

and you.

If you are asking for forever

If you are asking for forever,
I'll tell you that true love
doesn't need to ask for anything

because true connections find home
in each other
and when it happens, we will smile

at how easy this actually is.
You'll understand that nobody
has to chase anything.

If you're asking for forever,
I'll tell you that time doesn't exist,
that where we are now

is the same space our souls were
when they first met
at the beginning of time.

If you're asking for forever,
I'll ask you to close your eyes
and let your soul remind you

of when we first promised
to keep finding each other in all lifetimes,
when we were standing at the edge of time

playing with the stars.

If you are asking for forever,
I'll offer you a mirror
so you can see our souls

are already the reflection of one another
they always were,
they always will be.

Forever is yesterday,
forever is tomorrow,
forever is today.

Togetherness

I wasn't looking for love
for I didn't know what Love was before I met you.
How can you look for something if you don't know

what it is?

When all there ever was, was just pain and disappointment,
until you came along and showed me something different,
something I can hold on to.

You took all my beliefs that love was just pain
and loved them into something different.
Loving my darkness into light,

caressing my fears into droplets of hope.
Translating into a new language,
a new definition of togetherness.

Surrender

Unveil me slowly,
reveal what's underneath this armour.
Let me surrender to us.

Until the air becomes stale
and the world
stops turning.

Let this fire inside us burn as high
as the farthest star in the universe,
for this flame

is going to show us the way.
When all the stars will die
and darkness will be

all that is left,
let us be the only beacon of love

this world will ever see.

Love across lifetimes

"Why do you love me?"
You ask with innocent curiosity as you rest your head on my chest.
I look down as I breathe in the magnitude of
such a question.
And a glimpse of a soul-memory emerges,
as I see the bright bond that ties us together.
Of all the lifetimes we have travelled across time

always finding each other again.

How we searched for each other in other eyes,
of people we met along the journey.
Never quite right, always "not enough".

Finally understanding how we had to suffer such pain
to be together again.
So, I close my eyes and let these words

escape my breath:

"Because I can't remember a life when I didn't".

I knew you were the One

when my heart felt peace

before it could feel Love.

A momentary forever

And then there is that moment
        when every noise stops,
        when my heart feels at peace,
        when my mind feels clear.
Just a moment
        when I snuggle in your arms,
        and close my eyes,
        and I feel so safe I can
        surrender to a momentary
f o r e v e r.

Only good comes to us

Sometimes I don't know what to do with this overwhelming feeling of love and adoration. I feel like I am somehow devoted to you.

It's a strange feeling that makes me want to kneel just to catch my breath at the altar of this love, where candles are burning as high as the stakes are.

I close my eyes to re-centre and I breathe you in. Your breath washes over me like the most tender breeze of a summer we haven't yet had. We run towards our feelings like reckless children chasing waterfalls in a rainbow filled sky.

And I know, I know: I had been waiting for you.

Yet, fears knock on my door unexpectedly, I don't want to give them a seat at the table; they are not welcome here, not anymore.

For the first time in my life I surrender. I let go, to let you in. All of you.

There is space, I am making it. You hold my hand like you hold my heart: tenderly, securely, lovingly. There is no need to be afraid, all is well. Only good comes to us. Yet I wake up and you're not there next to me where I want to.

It's only for now, I know. But damn, I need you.

I miss your bones and your hand on my heart. The way you cup my face in your hands and pull my chin up to kiss me. The way you hold me so tight I feel like I am going to break, only each time you put me back together.

My mind slows down.

My thoughts are clear, my heart is calm.

You do this to me every time. It's no wonder I can't stay away from you,

for I just can't

not

love

you.

Becoming

I am becoming:
I don't know what,
or who, or how,
or when.

All I know is that
you are by my side
and whatever it is,
you are part of it.

You are part of me.

You are safe now

Winter has not yet left my heart,
demons from my past pay
an unexpected visit,

gripping my mind in chains
stronger than any love I have
for myself.

My words even struggle to form
sentences. It is difficult to make sense
of sounds when they drown in tears.

You place your hand on my heart,
and my hand on yours.
Your nose touches mine ever so slightly.

"*Breathe, my love*" – I hear you saying – "*You are safe now*".

I close my eyes, and I slowly feel
my heart beating in sync with yours.
My breath slows down.

My mind stops racing; I am breathing in love,
exhaling fear.

Even my demons leave the room
on their tiptoes.

Nothing else matters right now:
just our breath,
just the safety to be exactly who I am

with you.

Hold my heart

There is a way you hold my heart that I surrender to:
delicately, so it can breathe,
firmly, so it won't fall apart.

There is a way you hold my heart so sacredly
that even the Gods know
it is – finally – in the right hands.

Light

I can now finally see
how all the heartbreaks
were only stepping stones

that led me to the most beautiful light:

you, my love.

Y o u.

Forever

You kiss me and all I can do is
surrender
to this Love...

your touch,
your embrace,
our forever.

Undone

Your eyes consume me hungrily:
desire and passion dominate us like waves in a storm.
I let you in as your body moves slowly over mine.
Our breath fills the room as our minds shut down
the world outside;
your eyes are telling me a long story.
So, I look at you because I want to hear it...
hear it all,
right there,
without a single word
being spoken.

You

You are different.
    You listen when I don't speak.
    You talk with actions.
    You break down walls.

You bring love,
    oh, so much love.

With the right person,

the word "Commitment"

will sound like "Freedom".

The answer

I didn't know what I was asking until
you came along,
until I realised You are my answer:

to the doubts in my faith,
to the fears in my courage,
to the dreams in my sleep.

I didn't know what I was asking until I realised
You are my answer:

You are all my answers.

Still Change

The butterflies are not moving today;
their wings are firmly pinned to the
universal wall of change.

The newness is gone, and we are learning
to be in the day-to-day:
the kids schedule and the dogs'
arrangements.

The trains we need to jump on just to see
each other for an hour
in the midst between longing and
belonging.

The early nights where we just want to
collapse on the couch, too tired to even speak
as life keeps throwing waves against
a boat that is still too small.

It's learning to feel safe when we argue
and finding the courage to state our needs
without the fear of seeing our shadows
leaving in the dark.

It's learning that love doesn't go away
on the days the bed is half empty
or when words fail to leave our mouths.

It's giving each other the space to have a
bad day and still feeling connected.
It's having faith in time:

The only mirror to everything that is real.

Connected

The truth is,
I feel so connected to you
that I can hear a pin drop in the darkest
and the most remote corner
of your soul.

Happiness

Happiness is never just one big thing. It's watching your child becoming a young woman and finding her way in this world.

It's laughing at how the tram moves under their feet, making a squeaky noise, and they all laugh as if we had been doing this our entire lives.

Happiness it's stopping for a vanilla milkshake when your belly is already full, but you give in just because it's Saturday.

It's singing Disney songs in the car that you have heard a million times like it was the very first time.

Happiness is playing a silly game in your pyjamas at the end of a long day, counting your blessings in how those young eyes become bigger with every smile.

Happiness is never just one big thing. It folds in our ability to recognise the million parts of it and be grateful for each and every one of them.

Breathless

How beautiful
it is to have found a love where
I can breathe freely,
yet it still takes my breath
completely away.

Some days

Some days we are loved in the only way they can. Sometimes it's not wholly, it's not singing and dancing. Sometimes it lacks the words we want to hear.

There are days when the butterflies sleep tightly and refuse to move. These are the days that can carry profound anxiety and doubts.

People can love each other immensely and still not be aligned all the time. That is okay.

Just because you can't see the seeds in winter doesn't mean that flowers won't bloom in spring.

Surrender to the coldness of these days, trust that love doesn't go away when your hands are too tired to hold on.

Those are the days you will be the one being held.

Home

I used to dream about my house, of green plants and fluffy cushions.
Of a bed that is way too big, and a dim light that I can never figure out how to switch off.
I used to dream about everything that I have today, the only difference is that you are now the
one in the picture hung on the wall, with your arms wrapped around me.

And home now has a new meaning.

No matter how much you think

your light is out,

no matter how much you feel you

have nothing to give anymore,

you still light my world the

moment you are next to me.

Illusions

Ancient notions of time and space
are just an illusion when
"*Now*"
becomes the beginning of
"*Forever*".

Stories

Some stories are to be told,
        but some moments...
some moments are just to be *f e l t*.

With that Moon language

So admit something:
Why do you have to hear the words to believe
how worthy you are?

The wind doesn't ask the trees if they love it,
it just keeps going hugging them
day in and day out,
kissing the leaves until they are drunk of its love
and fall to rest.

The wind whispers secrets from other realms
only to ears ready to listen.

So admit something:
I don't have to tell you how much I love you
for my kisses to feel like love,
for my hugs to feel like the Earth is cocooning you,
for your hands to be worthy of being held.

Peace

And then one day it happens: what everyone had been talking about. My heart feels light, at peace. No longer shattered into a million pieces. And I don't even know how that is even possible. Not to live in chaos, second guessed and treated as an option.

I'm there, front row, my heart at the centre of infinite peace.
A future no longer made of ephemeral promises but only certainties.
A light that is there to stay, a warmth that my heart has been longing for eons.

I close my eyes at night, looking back with aching melancholy to all the doors that had to be shut to make space for us.
Of all the ground that had to be burned so that new soil could grow.
Of the ocean of tears that I had to swim through on days I thought I'd drown.
There could have never been any other way.

And now I know why.

And if I were to choose all over again, I'd choose all the heartaches again,
because they only led me to You, my love.

Part 3

Refraction of Time

Above us

The wolf

He came to see me in my sacred garden today. His blue eyes and white fur always mesmerize me. A sense of sorrow emerges slowly. I don't have much time left.

He places his head on my lap and we sit quietly together for a while.
My eyes close, absorbing the purplish light of the garden, restoring a little bit of energy.
Letting go of the expectations and images of a longer life.

My soul is ready to detach from my body as I say goodbye to everything I've ever known.

Wolf is not speaking, but he is carrying a message of resilience and a gentle reassurance, somehow knowing I need more than that.
And yet the most simple message is the most powerful, and exactly what I needed.

My time here on Earth is finished.
I need to go home.

Souls know not

limits or boundaries.

I'll find you again, my love,

across lifetimes.

Next life is ours,

I promise.

The beginning

Where am I?
A light is pulling me up,
and all I can do is surrender to this force
and let go for the first time,
fully and without resistance,
leaving behind all that this body has ever known.
This is not an ending like I've always thought;
there is no sorrow,
there is no pain.
I no longer have a body;
my soul glistens in a bright light
that swirls into a million stardust particles.
I am being pulled into another dimension:
I no longer have eyes, yet I see everything.
I no longer have a heart, yet I feel peace.
I no longer have ears, yet I hear the sweet echoes
of all my loved ones patiently waiting for me.

I know now
    I have just come
        home.

Karmic purpose

There is a sense of surrender to everything that has ever
happened in this life on Earth. Joy carried pain in her
pocket, and pain carried wisdom on her back.
Courage never walked alone and love was
what always connected everything.

There has never been anything that has happened
that hasn't taught me something:

Creating life and being the teacher of new souls incarnated
in bodies of who today are wonderful women standing in
their power carrying the ancient light of divine
feminine energy through this world.

Heartbreak, cursing and curling in a ball crying over lost
love, opening my heart again and crying out of joy
getting lost in the wisdom of finding myself
over and over again.

Time is the only mirror that can reflect the true lessons
on offer when ears are ready to listen and hearts are
ready to mend; love carried me through each and
every moment, especially the toughest ones.

And it is only now that I see
the magnificence of it all.

A message from the guides

You were swimming in the most beautiful river.
You had a boat full of flowers and life-boats.
Waters were still until they weren't.
The storm rocked the boat so much
that you felt you fell in the river.
Do you remember how you held onto that branch
for so long, my child, for so long.
Suffocating at each wave. Relentless.
You didn't let go, all your energies were focussed
on surviving the storm.

But do you remember what happened
when you were holding on thinking you couldn't anymore?
You thought if you let go you would drown.
You'd fall and hurt yourself even more.
When the last wave arrived – *was it was the river or your tears, there was no way of discerning* – your hands let go of the branch. There was no way to hold on anymore, and the water carried you down the river.
You let go of everything you knew.

The breeze of the wind swept away the tears, the water carried you like a lifeboat of its own.
You allowed yourself to smile, to surrender, to enjoy the crazy ride down the rapids.
And then you finally saw how at the bottom
everything was still.

Everything had a purpose.
Everything made sense.
Because you let go of that branch, my child.
Because you decided to ride the waves,
not only you survived,
you came *back to life.*

Everything is clear

There could have never been another way – you and I were destined to collide, I can understand now as I read the soul contract we made, my love.

I am waiting here patiently for your return home as you finish your time on Earth. I can see and feel you from here, and you are doing such an incredible job at keeping everything together in my absence.

Everything is so beautiful and peaceful here, I can't even say that I *feel* love because I am *made* of love: pure energy and deep understanding for everything that is, everything that was, everything that will be.

I have been shown my own unique Tapestry of The Oneness and how I decided with the guides which path I was going to choose, which lessons I had to learn, and at what point we could meet. And now I remember everything so well. The intuition that guided us when we met, the pull we felt when our hands first touched, that electricity and sense of familiarity, that's what you and I agreed at the beginning of time, when we promised we'd find each other.

I have met our sould family. I was shown the role they played in our lives on Earth, who took the role of the ones breaking our respective hearts and I understood why it had to be that way. There was no anger. We smiled at each other with deep understanding and gratitude for a role well played that served a higher purpose.

I wish I could show you how clear everything is now.

Nothing happened by chance, especially the hurt and heart-break and despair. Those were the moments we grew the most, and opened the Bridge of Incidents that allowed us to find each other, over and over again.

I have learned the true meaning of Love in this life, of compassion and how I was always enough for myself. I was shown how in previous lives I had failed to learn that lesson, and that's the reason I chose a more difficult one, this time.

The time it will take you to come here will feel like a heartbeat here for me and probably many years for you; I will rest and restore my energy and we will all welcome you, when the time has come.

There is no urgency here, no pressure, no anxiety – only love and warmth and peace.

I will wait for you by the stars, the same ones where we said goodbye the first time when we went to Earth; you'll know by the time you get here and you will recognise me. We don't have bodies here, but you will immediately feel pulled towards me because you and I are made from the same soul: that's why in each other's presence we always felt like home.

We always will.

Everything in life comes back
transformed
recharged
changed
like pain
like love
like wisdom

Acknowledgments

Emmanuel – my brother, best friend and partner in crime in all my journeys and adventures. Thank you for another stunning job of formatting this book.

Wren Coaching – Ren – my sister and soul companion whose coaching sessions helped me see so clearly I wanted to be an author a few years ago, I wouldn't be here today without you.

My beautiful girls – Eli and Erica – yes, mamma wrote another book! And, this time, I'm really glad you liked the title. Thank you for the endless cups of peppermint tea, hugs and kisses.

Franco Cardiello – my dearest friend and fellow author – for spending hours on zoom reminding me how to alchemise pain into poetry and for helping me figure out the titles of the chapters when I was totally stuck.

Stefanie Briar – my editor and friend, thank you for the guidance, support, and meticulous work in bringing my vision to life.

Mark Croasdale – for being the first set of eyes on the first draft of the manuscript and helping me untangle the story so I could see clearly which direction to take.

To the man who inspired my love poems, thank you for showing me what being in love truly felt like.

To the advanced readers group – you are awesome and I am forever in your debt!

To my fantastic readers on all my social media platforms, I wouldn't be here today without your constant support.

About the Author

Barbara Gianquitto is a poet, writer and author of the best-selling poetry collections "4:04am Thoughts" and "Awakening of the Heart".

Listed as one of the top 10 authors to look out for in 2023, Barbara writes about love and heartbreak, self-discovery and healing with a soft, open and unique voice that has gathered the interest of over 60 thousand readers on social media across the world and a feature at the BBC national radio.

As a graduate in communication and psychology and a Neuro-Linguistic practitioner and coach, Barbara's passion has always been in the power of words and communication, inspiring her readers to dive deeper into their own power and self-discovery.

Barbara also writes for children, her brand new children's book "Loretta and the Monday morning blues" focuses on validating children's feelings to better equip them for the future, gently teaching them how it's always okay to feel what we feel, and that happiness can be found in the smallest things.

Born and raised in Italy, Barbara currently lives in the United Kingdom with her family and a grumpy cat; she drinks far too much coffee, follows the Moon in all its phases, and is a hopeless romantic.

You can find more about Barbara's work and upcoming projects on her website ***www.barbaragianquitto.com***.

Words are all we have in this world.

We should use them more often.

@barbara.gianquitto.author
@BarbaraNgianquitto
@bgianquitto
@barbara.gianquitto

Printed in Great Britain
by Amazon

28049511R00092